HOW TO TRADE FOREX

How To Make $ Millions In Forex Trading

By Chuck Thomas

Copyright © 2014 by Chuck Thomas

All rights reserved. No part of this book may be reproduced or transmitted in any form or by any means, electronic or mechanical, including photocopying, recording, or by an information storage and retrieval system - except by a reviewer who may quote brief passages in a review to be printed in a magazine or newspaper - without permission in writing from the publisher.

ISBN-13: 978-1495989421
Create Space
ISBN-10: 1495989429

Printed in the United States of America

CONTENTS

Foreword   5

1. Accurate Forex Signals   6
2. Most Accurate Signals   9
3. Forex Trading Robot   11
4. Forex Rates   13
5. Learn Online Trading   15
6. Forex Trading Companies   17
7. Forex Trading System   19
8. Global Forex   22
9. Forex Trading Tools   24
10. Forex Trading Programs   26
11. Learn Online Trading   28
12. Forex Articles   30
13. Auto Forex Robot   32
14. Easy Forex Signals   34
15. Forex Global   37
16. Forex Signals Auto   39
17. Forex Trade   42
18. Forex Trading Account   44
19. Forex Trading Basics   47
20. Forex Trading Blog   49
21. Forex Trading Chart   51
22. Forex Trading Courses   53
23. Trading Forex Online   55
24. Best Accurate Forex   57
25. Online Forex Trading   61
26. Genuine Online Trading   63
27. Forex Trading News   65
28. Online Trading Tools   68
29. Forex Exchange   71

30. Forex Trading Demo	73
31. Forex Trading Indicators	75
32. Forex Trading Tutorial	78
33. Forex Trading Strategy	80
34. Best Forex Trading	82
35. Forex Trading Guide	84
36. How to trade	86
37. Auto Forex Trading System	88
38. Easy Forex	92
39. Forex Trading Forex	95
40. Forex Trading Forum	98
41. Forex Trading Scams	100
42. Learn Forex Trading	103
43. Learn Trading Online	105
44. Online Currency Trading	107
45. Managed Forex Trading	109
46. Online Trading Broker	111
47. Auto Forex Traders	114
48. Forex Trading Tips	116
49. Forex Trading Education	118
50. Forex Trading Seminar	120
51. Forex Trading Platforms	122
52. Online Trading Scams	124
53. Online Trading System	127
54. Forex Market Trading	129
55. Forex Trading	131
56. Learn Currency Trading	133
57. Trading Spot Forex	135

FOREWORD

I have put together this Book to dispel the myth about the $4 Trillion a day Forex market. And how it operates, and how to make millions if you trade correctly, and how to get the needed Forex Education and training, that is needed to be on top of your game. You need to know when and when not to employ a Forex Broker. You must also, be aware of the many Forex scams online.

Many people jump into the online trading market to earn some extra cash, looking for less work, but the truth still stands that the online trading is not for the lazy. It demands some complex work of the mind, and quite a great deal of data analysis. When developing your own Forex trading plan, just be sure that your plan works for you and you stay regimented, so that you can increase your prospects of fulfillment.

Software called Auto Robot has been created, so you do not need to sit in front of the computer to make transactions in the forex market. You can buy auto robots and this can work for you. There are some auto robots that offer more than 95 percent accuracy in the transactions. Therefore you can trust them. However, such software is not free from limitations.

1

Accurate Forex Signals

For Making Money and Maximize your profits

Forex traders often use accurate forex signals, usually on a subscription basis. Online you can find some of the best advice and strategies for making it big on the Forex market using the best accurate Forex Trading Signals, so be sure to check it out! The information is usually sent via email.

Even newbie's can succeed in the market given a modicum of experience and a reliable signal. This can be on a weekly, monthly or even annual scheme.

The garnering of suitable and valid information, not to mention the actual quantity needed to make any kind of reasonable assessment to trade successfully, would not be possible to most people who trade.

Apart from the complex new trading platforms available these days, there are expert advisers for it, and several types of scripts and a large number of signaling service providers available.

There is a remarkable amount of hi-tech in these times, which has birthed several strategies, auto forex trading systems, forex trading Robot and forex trading indicators to name a few.

The increasing use of accurate forex signals are due to the hugely complicated and rapidly changing nature of the foreign currency exchange industry.

The signals data, which is based on much careful research of the currency movements, is collated and broadcast to subscribers suggesting to them the entry and exit points on certain currencies.

In this chapter, the spotlight will be on the most accurate forex signals and the validity of signaling services generally.

Traders in foreign exchange can be found in almost any location on the planet. This will provide the potential client to test drive so to speak the service and test it in an actual trade in real time.

A great deal of currency is exchanged and traded on the basis of the accuracy of these signals. Some signals service companies offer a trial subscription.

One of the main advantages is that a quality signal service provider will give the investor a marked advantage through the information that under normal circumstances, only an experienced professional trader would have knowledge of.

Hedge Managers are responsible for this. Most are happy to pay for a service that claims to help. Trading with the Accurate Forex Signals can be a very profitable venture; the carefully researched fiscal data is transmitted to subscribing traders.

Clients whether individual or institutional receive the most accurate forex signals possible, sent to their respective online trading platforms. The idea is for the investor to have data to enable him to make a sound decision as possible on when to place and exit a trade.

Naturally, the companies who broadcast them are extremely cautious to ensure the data is as accurate as possible prior to being sent. Signals are meant for use at a particular point in time and are sent out in real-time, delayed by several minutes normally.

2

Most Accurate Signals

The indication is known as exist and enter indication and it is mainly according to the proper analysis and research of financial information from many sources.

The main idea of this is to help the traders to make a good decision on what type of currency to trade, and when to sell or purchase a currency. Information offered by these indications can be emails instantly to the traders, who will check his ideas and will act accordingly.

A signal service organization will not send the wrong information because the subscribers will pay a fee on monthly or yearly basis. There are billions of dollars traded on the foreign currency exchange market and therefore the signal firms are to be careful to give correct and precise signals to the investors.

When to purchase or sell

These accurate signals are good for the right time but sometimes can be delayed by many minutes. There are some people use forex charts or forex trading signals which helps the trader when to purchase or sell. These signals will talk about the change and trends in the market.

It is very simple and easy to understand how to do the foreign currency exchange but is very hard to execute it. Institutional and individual traders are looking at accurate signals that are sent to the trading platforms.

The main reason why

The main reason why most of the investors are depending on the trading signals because forex trading is a difficult business, only when the trader collects all the needed information to trade, in order to be successful in the forex market.

You will also have the opportunity to receive a trial period with the signaling companies. It helps you to inspect the speed and right data you are getting instantly. The main advantage on receiving this signals is, a trader by not considering his knowledge cannot perform trading effectively.

3

Forex Trading Robot

Forex trading Robot software is found helpful to traders and among them includes trading robot. To them, using a robot is advantageous because of the many wonder jobs it can do to help the trader earn.

The trading robot trades on behalf of the trader. This permits the trader to do other activities he/she wishes to do. There is no need for you to baby sit your computer for long hours just to trade. Since the software is a robot, it is not susceptible to any feelings which may affect the trading process. They are not affected in anyway if pips are becoming huge or when the value of your currency pairs is going down.

Excitements accompanying trading

Using them may relieve you from worries, panics, frustrations, and excitements accompanying trading. You need to understand that the downside of being subjected to this kind of feelings affects you negatively. You might trade unwisely until you may later find out you have no investment left in your account.

Another advantage of using trading robot is their accuracy in trading which sometimes cannot be beaten by human mind. It cannot be denied that traders could be distracted with their surroundings no matter how they try to be attentive.

Robots on the other hand have the concentration all the time even during the wee hours in the morning. Once installed correctly, it may trade at the right time you wish it to buy and sell your currency pairs.

Forex robots also sticks

Forex robots also stick to the plan which is an excellent move. Forex trading is a business venture requiring disciplined players.

If you do not possess such personality, it is best to use forex trading robots however you need to check to make sure there are no interruptions with your internet and electricity connections. Any disturbances with these may mean a great lose.

4

Forex Rates

Depending on what currency you are trading, and which currencies you are trading with and to, they are going to vary based on the current exchange rates, it dependent upon various factors in the market and the economy. The exchange rate from the dollar to pounds or to euros, or to any other currency being used in the forex market, will depend upon economic factors as well as current rates for the prices of stock, and the currency that they are originally traded in. So, the rates for a US based stock might vary from the rates of a stock based in the UK or any other countries which are traded on the market.

Additionally, the rates are going to fluctuate as the economy does. Since the dollar is weaker than most currencies, the rates for American traders might be lower than that of traders in the UK or in Australia.

Forex market and stock conditions

Therefore, keeping up with current economic trends, and knowing what is going on in your economy, and the value of the currency you are trading with, are also variables that traders must be aware of, in order for them to know what the current are as well.

Knowing the general forex market and stock conditions, as well as being aware with what is going on in the economy and with the value of your home currency, are things forex traders must know in order to keep up with the rates, and to know what is going on with their stock trades. The more you study the forex rates and economic factors, and the more time a trader takes in learning about these rates, the greater they are going to do on the market, and the greater the potential for higher earnings.

5

Learn Online Trading

Learn Online Trading, with the continuous increase of interest of the people on the internet market, the growth of online trading has increased many folds.

As a new trader, a person has to seriously consider learning trading, if he wants to take the right decisions at the right time and more effectively. An abundant amount of knowledge is required to develop a trading strategy that can help in cash inflow.

The first thing is to know exactly what is online trading. Online trading can be defined as a deal between two persons, where one person is selling and another is buying, and there is a contract that the prices of the goods and products remain unaffected throughout the whole process.

Online trading market

Even if many people jump into the online trading market to earn some extra cash out of less work, but the truth still stands that the online trading is not for the lazy. It demands some complex work of the mind and quite a great deal of data analysis.

There are many websites available on the internet, who serve the process of online trading and there are also websites which cater to provide the right knowledge to the online traders to carry out the process efficiently.

The most famous online trading

One of the most famous online trading business companies is forex trading, which serves both the purpose of providing materials to learn online trading as well as providing an environment to do online trading.

While almost everyone can do online trading, most people do jump into the trading business without even learning the correct way to trade currencies. This results in losing a huge amount of money in trading. To learn trading, it takes quite a great deal of time and one should have the patience and the strategy to make a huge profit out of this online trading business.

6

Forex Trading Companies

When trading on the forex market, one must seek out the services of genuine and reliable companies to service their trades and exchanges in the market.

The main reason that choosing those companies which are genuine and reliable is that they will properly do the conversion on the currency you are trading with.

Since the forex market deals with all forms of currency, these companies will convert your currency, to ensure you are getting the highest possible value for it when making a trade or purchase.

Take the current highest value

As the currencies are subject to various comparative values, the companies chosen will take the current highest value, to ensure you will get the biggest returns on your transactions.

If, on the other hand, you had to rely on an outside source to convert the exchange rate, you might be faced with the possibility of getting less value than what your currency is currently valued at.

When selecting the companies to use for services online, consumers have to take the time to compare all of them.

There are scammers out there

As there are hundreds of companies to choose from, there are scammers out there, and if you do not properly research the information that is available, it is probable that you will choose the wrong trading companies to convert your trades online.

There are reliable, legitimate private trading companies that you can choose to trade with. But, as a trader, it is up to you how much time you are going to take in researching the forex trading companies on the web.

If you are willing to take the time and effort to do the work, it is very possible to find genuine companies to trade with, in turn, getting the highest values for your currency and the highest returns on trades and transactions you make.

7

Forex Trading System

Forex trading system, when you choose to make your individual Fx dealing method, there will be one additional thing that you will need to think about.

Eventually, you might need to be ready to figure out specific variations, while doing positive these variations are genuine. What you need to maintain in mind when developing your individual Forex trading System plan, is the fact that you're actually creating a strategy which will execute available trades for you, as an individual or buyer.

Once you have a Forex Trading System that performs for you, you must remember to keep with the program. Do not make the mistake of ditching your program if you want to engage in options that are perceptibly more successful, as this lack of discipline will dramatically increase your possibilities of disaster. In order for a Forex trading plan to work effectively, you must be constant.

You need to consider

You will be required to identify what exactly performs the best for you, just before you choose to trade live. You need to consider the period in which you will be operating in and the quantity of investment that you are willing to put at probability, when you start dealing. Normally, the going frequent cross-over program is advised to establish versions.

The going regular cross-over program involves two going earnings, which together figure out the times in which you should buy and sell, The family associate strength catalog (RSI) you to use, if you want to either validate or reject versions.

When creating your own currency software program, make sure you also figure out the stage of anger that you'll want to put out, using the returning into and leaving of each of your investments.

If you are investors would delay until the candles have shut for the currency sets they will work with, if you would like to hold more balance when coming into investments.

Your own Forex software system

Finally, if you create your own Forex software system, you must create a program that works for you and to be frequent with whatever performs for you. Of course, some Forex trading techniques depend on the person individual or buyer. Some dealing strategies are however, recommended for nearly all of traders and investors in the Forex trading market:

The going regular cross-over program for determining variations and the family member durability catalog for confirming or doubting variations. In most cases necessary to figure out the quantity of investment that are willing to put at possibility, as well as the level of anger that you will want to put out, with the returning into and leaving of each your investments.

When developing your own Forex trading plan, just be sure that your plan works for you and you stay regimented, so that you can increase your prospects of fulfillment.

8

Global Forex

Global Forex trading is the foreign market exchange involving currencies of countries around the world, almost all countries in the world, which is usually represented by the company or their biggest banks, participating in that activity.

In the forex market, we will find the money is sold and bought based on the value of the currency at the time. This is done to create balance in the currency markets around the world. This activity is similar to the stock market in a country, but in a much larger scale because it involves almost all countries in the world.

There are some countries, which became the main trade center as Tokyo, New York, or London, but on the other hand, there are several locations that do not occur trading. Currency prices in these activities are always changing and different every day.

Invest huge amounts

If you want to invest huge amounts of money, then you should watch more closely and learn it first because you could lose your money. You can get involve in currency trading activities by contacting a broker who knows what will happen before the general public, and know the secrets of business for making money in Global Forex. Another thing you can do is get all the information about the company and transactions online via the internet.

Frequently traded currencies

Frequently traded currencies in global trading, usually has a symbol consisting of three letters representing the countries and currencies that are traded.

You can find that the Japanese yen is the JPY, U.S. dollar is the USD; British pound is the GBP; Euro is the EUR, and much more. Activity that often occurs is a trade between EUR and USD, USD and JPY, and GBP and USD. Trafficking occurred throughout the day and all night from markets around the world. Time zone also affects how forex trading takes place in which one country open the trade and another closed.

9

Forex Trading Tools

There are thousands of Forex Trading Tools available to the trader, the problem this presents is the task of choosing the right tool for ones trading need.

For any trader to run a business smoothly they may need things like a computer, this should be fast enough with reliable internet connection.

They also need good foreign currencies and charting software with the right type of data that one can use to study currency movements in good times.

The tools required

Some of the tools required for efficient trading include; the Meta trader, it is a very useful tool and one of the most advanced in the market;

This is because it enables the trader to analyze, organize, compare and customize all the trading information available to them. With reliable internet connection, this information can be done real time basis.

Another tool that is necessary for efficient Forex trading is the signal software; this can work with any market and any time frame. It also has the ability to design frame work and proper methods along clear entry or exit regulations to the market. It is one of the most important tools of forex trading.

Another forex trading tool

Another forex tool is the strategy builder, this helps in creating a good strategy in the forex market. It is very important in identifying those trades that are likely to make high profits by including effective and powerful money management techniques.

There are also trend analyzers; this uses one indicator to analyze the market. It predicts the expected market changes based on the overall behavior over some duration of time.

It is for these tools that make forex trading smooth and without them, trading may be unbearable to many of the traders. Failure to use these tools, one may not be able to analyze the market properly and may end up incurring losses in their trade.

10

Forex Trading Programs

Forex trading programs, it is a common knowledge that forex trading is tricky and unpredictable. As such, if you are a beginner, you are advised to attend forex trading training.

The main reason for this is to spare yourself from the list of failed investors. Figures show that almost 90% of new traders who are struggling to make it in the forex trading business are their failure to learn trading programs. Although, it is not a 100 percent guarantee, attending trading programs increases your chance of survival in the industry.

Learn forex trading

Forex trading programs comes in different forms. There are those designed for starters, advance, and a program designed specifically to teach the use of trading tools. Anybody interested in learning forex trading does not need to travel anywhere else since programs are offered online.

Individuals who prefer to take it offline may do so because the program can be offered through a modular method. Programs are also designed in a way that topics are divided weekly making it possible for participants to choose the lesson they wish to attend, only.

However, if you intend to learn the most bulk of the forex trading, you can do it so by attending the entire course.

The forex programs

Most often, the forex programs are not merely lectures or paper-pencil method. In most cases, lessons are accompanied with videos for demonstrating purposes. This is most applicable when learning the how Do's of robots and other software. The right timing of trading, how to trade, and the potentials of every currency are all thought during the course.

Although, you can learn on your own, it makes a difference when you learn the programs from experts as they know the step by step guide in becoming a successful trader. Sometimes the secret of forex business resides in the trading programs which are not readily available online or offline.

11

Learn Online Trading

Learn Online Trading, with the continuous increase of interest of the people on the internet market, the growth of online trading has increased many folds.

As a new trader, a person has to seriously consider learning trading, if he wants to take the right decisions at the right time and more effectively. An abundant amount of knowledge is required to develop a trading strategy that can help in cash inflow.

The first thing is to know exactly what is online trading. Online trading can be defined as a deal between two persons, where one person is selling and another is buying, and there is a contract that the prices of the goods and products remain unaffected throughout the whole process.

Online trading market

Even if many people jump into the online trading market to earn some extra cash out of less work, but the truth still stands that the online trading is not for the lazy. It demands some complex work of the mind and quite a great deal of data analysis.

There are many websites available on the internet, who serve the process of online trading and there are also websites which cater to provide the right knowledge to the online traders to carry out the process efficiently.

The most famous online trading

One of the most famous online trading businesses is forex trading, which serves both the purpose of providing materials to learn online trading as well as providing an environment to do online trading.

While almost everyone can do online trading, most people do jump into the trading business without even learning the correct way to trade currencies. This results in losing a huge amount of money in trading. To learn trading, it takes quite a great deal of time and one should have the patience and the strategy to make a huge profit out of this online trading business.

12

Forex Articles

Whether you are already trading in the forex market, or whether you plan on entering the market, reading various articles will help traders determine what are the best tips, techniques, and types of stocks to buy into.

Depending on the author of the articles, and depending on the types of articles one reads they are going to find several different pieces of information, on a wide variety of topics.

There are several individuals in the market (such as traders) who will write articles about their experience in the market; there are also experts in the market, who study the trends and problems in the forex market, who will write interpretative articles to help traders determine when, and if they should enter the market.

Reading all types of articles, on all topics, and by all types of authors, can be a valuable tool for a trader who is planning on engaging in the forex market.

No matter which articles you read

No matter which articles you read, they must be written by a reputable and reliable source in the forex market, and they must be aimed at the types of stocks and trades you are planning on engaging in as a trader in the market.

The more articles one reads, the more in depth knowledge they are going to receive about the market, from experts and from other traders.

There are several types of forex articles that can aid a trader into determining when and whether or not they should enter the forex market. There are also articles which will help the traders choose which stocks to buy.

What to avoid, and other valuable information. No matter what your information and knowledge levels are, reading articles can always be beneficial to a trader who is entering the forex market.

13

Auto Forex Robot

People often ask what an auto forex Robot is. There are many investors who reap higher level of profits by investing in the foreign currency market.

As the exchange rate between two currencies keep on changing due to marketing forces, the investors can either gain or loss money depending upon the changes in the value of currencies. The investors can invest in foreign exchange market by sitting at home with a computer and internet connection.

Many people complain that they need to have a close watch at the exchange rate by looking at the computer monitor all the time. This has in fact led many people to think that they are spending their valuable time in front of computers.

As a solution to this problem, software called auto robot has been created. You do not need to sit in front of the computer to make transactions in forex market. You can buy auto robots and this will work for you.

There are some auto robots that offer more than 95 percent accuracy in the transactions. Therefore you can trust them. However, such software is not free from limitations.

The Auto Forex Robot

The auto robots can make calculations only on the basis of statistical data. But, as the market is highly volatile to demand and supply conditions there is no assurance that investors can only gain by analyzing the past information.

Hence, investors should consider such risks due to the use of auto robots before they use any free software. It should be noted that your money is handled by software on the basis of statistical data.

Hence, although such trading systems are good in many ways, one should be very careful not to use free software. Whatever may be the case, it is true that there are many people who use more efficient auto robots and earn profits.

14

Easy Forex Signals

How Forex Signals Work:

Easy forex signals are the fundamental verbal codes in trading forex. Easy forex signals are used by the traders as signs for both good and bad times in forex trading.

They have been used by them like factors for making decision in the forex trading. These indicators are communicated from broker to another agent by telegram or telegraph in the olden days. Today the forex growth can be seen on the internet. The investors can make their own indicators to match their online forex trading.

Beginners and brokers of forex trading may use the services of best forex automated trading firm to receive a hold of a better forex indicator generator. It will create forex indications according to the behavioral methods of various currency ratings.

A best way to get the forex automated trading signals is by viewing the customer review on the internet. Users who had bad experience with the bad one can give their comments by keeping in the mind that another person should not be cheated like them.

Online searches for these types of reviews are simple and easy. All these easy forex signals are just like a proxy systems for the trader who could not check the currency rate. They are indicators of normal trading possibilities and these are algorithmic methods that have been proved in the effective forex trades. These signals will help to make decisions or suggest the trader to take further actions.

Using these signals by the traders help

Using these signals by the traders help them to make profits by checking the currency rate. Besides all the other aspects of foreign trading many wise decisions are to be considered here and these will be highly unpredictable.

Often the investors should have a rock heart as there may be lot of changes that can happen and these will in turn affect the benefits one gets. There are chances like the wise people who are well versed will be going upside down and these will be leading to careful losses.

However, with careful patience one can get the benefits where they have lost. And thus hurry will never get any return in the case of forex trading. Thus, have a bright and successful career with the forex trading.

15

Forex Global

The forex global trading is nothing but, buying a currency as well as selling another currency to the same broker, or to a market that is dealing with all of these trade issues.

There is a particular market called interbank market, and this will be used for making all such dealings. Here, the noticeable thing is that the currencies will vary depending on the condition of the nation in terms of economical benefits.

Forex training provides people a big opportunity to make money from forex trading. It is dangerous for one to use, so it is essential to know that certain things as trial forex trading permits people to practice the trading of forex. Even, when you use trial account, you should take the trading with dedication from the beginning. It is good to open trades, one and then another one. It is difficult and important not to trade too many numbers of trades at one time.

Making profits in the forex trading

When you have a strong position by making profits in the forex trading, then you can easily move to another position. Always keep your eye on the market fluctuation,

Political change which is the essential factors that influence the currency money. Administrating the risk is very important for making profit in the forex global trading.

Only when you know and understand about risk management you can be able to earn cash by forex purchasing. All methods contain both merits and demerits and you have to be careful.

If the leverage is to minimum you will not be able to make more money even when you have a successful system.

Therefore, risk should be maximized for the methods. You can avail between 1 to 5 percent of the funds on each trade. Use only about 5 percent when you lose the full balance and usually the more capital in the account, the less capital will be danger on one trade. Forex trading is the best way to make money fast in the short period of time, but you should know the basic things before trading.

16

Forex Signals Auto

Forex signals auto money systems helps the traders to make money.

The forex signals money patterns has been used by many traders effectively for years. It is a different method that specializes in the forex trading market. Forex trading market is the big financial chances for the people who are interested to do forex trading.

The forex signals auto money methods are made to assist navigate you by the big market. This system is created to offer you with the trading indications every day. It avails indications which are generated on three various time frames to offer you the best trading indications.

They will offer with the intra-day signs which will give you the several various chances to trade every day. They will also give you everyday indications which come once a day. You can easily access the weekly indications which will give you the trades that performed each single week. The weekly indications will be big trades that focus for big profits. The intra-day indications will provide you with information for consistent profits coming daily.

This system uses the new techniques to give you signals. They use a group of experts that are included with statisticians, mathematicians and specialized forex traders to discover the best possibilities every day, they will post the trading indications to the back office, hence, that they will easily found when you require them.

You can just login to the back office and receive the indications when you want to trade. You will open a trading platform on the internet; you will trade on the platform and wait for the money to come in. This method offers an effective winning percentage when compared to other forex methods that are available in the market.

Make large amounts each day

You can easily make large amounts of money each day. You should remember that it will require capital for trading to begin forex signals auto trading. You have to invest your money in the other currencies to make profit.

You are buying a contract of a specific amount of a currency and believing to get benefit from the difference in the rate between the currencies. You can close the trading when you sell the currency at a higher price. It offers you with the profit on the trade.

The money which you can earn based highly on the investment you made on the trade. Hence, the more money contains in your account, the more money you can make on the trade at a time. Forex auto money is basically a software system which offers you indications when to enter or exit and when to purchase and sell the currency in the market.

When you want to use this system you should have a computer and internet connection. Secondly, it will require money to trade with the currencies. Thirdly, you have to select the auto money offering website to subscribe and to use the services. There are number of websites that provides demo services for certain amount of days at a lower cost. It will be more useful for the investors to order a trial services and to check whether it is useful or not.

17

Forex Trade

A great deal of people has heard of the stock exchange but confuse it with forex trade. Forex is similar to stock exchange except currency is used. The volume is greater than stocks and bonds together. It also comes with a high risk as with any other forms of trading. However, forex can yield a high return.

The most beneficial thing about forex is it applies a margin which doesn't require the full amount to purchase the currency. A thousand dollars can return the investor $100000 permitting a profit with very little upfront costs.

Forex allows anyone to be investors and not just big companies. Those wanting to get started with trade are wise seeking advice from forums. The secret to understanding forex is knowledge.

The investor needs to select a system

The investor needs to select a system. A system refers to software, a course, or especially contrived technique. Many systems are available so the investor should choose one that suits them, and ask questions before making a purchase like how long they have been in operation.

It is wise to read testimonials and find out if a free trial is offered. Chat rooms and forums will give the investor an idea on what works. Experts believe an effective system is the foundation for successful trading, as it guides the investors on each trading situation.

A broker will also be needed

A broker will also be needed to help with transactions in forex trade. When a trader is looking for a broker, they need to ask about their credentials, leverage, and spread.

It is an important factor in the amount of money they can make. Transactions can be handled with no broker. An investor should get educated on analysis, master strategies, and have a competitive edge. A trader will improve their success if they do their research. They must be prepared for profits and losses.

18

Forex Trading Account

Getting started with online forex trading account is pretty easy these days. With just a small amount of capital and an internet connection, you can open an account with one of the many online forex trading platforms in a matter of a few minutes.

There are various types of accounts, all with varying options and features. Here are some of the most common.

Demo accounts

These are usually offered at no cost to enable newbie forex traders to practice and fine tune their skills. Demo accounts are usually fully fledged just like the ordinary accounts, but rather than risk real money, the traders practice with virtual money.

While demo accounts are increasingly being used by forex trading platforms all across the internet to attract new traders, you should check whether the respective broker is in compliance with the applicable regulations. For instance, in the USA, you should check to see that the broker is compliant with NFA regulatory standards.

The perfect trading accounts

Mini and micro accounts

These are the perfect trading accounts for newbie traders wanting to move beyond experimenting with virtual money. They allow the traders an opportunity to gain confidence while at the same time risking relatively low capital.

While mini accounts can be opened with as little as $1,000, traders can open a micro account for as low as 1$. Mini forex trading account can be run with a 10,000 units which renders their minimum fluctuation equivalent to 1$. A micro trading account on the other hand typically come with a size of 1,000 units which means that their minimum pip fluctuation is *equivalent to $0.10.*

Standard trading account

As the name suggests, this is the most common forex trading account. The traders usually have access currency lots to the tune of $100,000. This of course doesn't mean that the traders will have to deposit a capital of $100,000 upfront.

Leverage of 100:1

At the leverage of 100:1 that is the most commonly used, a forex trader only needs to deposit $1000. Every pip is worth $10 and this means that a shift of 100 pips in a trading day rolls down to a total gain of $1,000 for the lot traded.

On the downside however, it follows that the risk involved is equally higher since a negative pip move by $100 also means total loss of $1,000.

Irrespective of which forex trading account you choose, you should first of all practice with forex trading before diving in head first. In other words, you should take the time to gain experience using virtual money typically provided before risking with your hard earned real money.

19

Forex Trading Basics

People often ask what forex market is, and what the forex trading basics are. Forex or foreign Exchange refers to the foreign currency. We know that countries have their own domestic currencies in their geographical area.

However, in the international market, currencies of various countries can be traded just like any other commodities. Investors buy the currency when its value in terms of another currency is low and sell it when its value is higher.

There are many investors who make profits by investing in forex market. As the exchange rate between two currencies always keep on changing due to various factors, the investors can either make profit or suffer from loss due to the changes in the value of currencies.

In short, Investment can either leads to earn profit or suffer from loss. Therefore it is better to know the basics before you think of making investment in forex market.

Currencies can either appreciate or depreciate

Currencies can either appreciate or depreciate the value in terms of other currencies. Appreciation means increase and depreciation means decrease in the value of one currency in terms of another currencies. This change in the value lays the basis for making the transaction in the forex market. Let us make it more clearly with an example. Suppose there are two currencies, X and Y and further let us assume that one 'X' is equal to two 'Y'.

In this situation, if you buy the currency 'X' in order to exchange it with 'Y' then you make profit when the value of currency X increases in terms of currency Y. That means you can buy more than two 'Y' with one 'X'. The changes in the value of currency X will be your profit. You may wonder how to make the transactions in forex market. As the technology is more advanced now, you can invest in forex market via online. That makes the investment easier.

20

Forex Trading Blog

There are several online forex trading blog sites that one can visit, prior to entering the forex market, in order to read about one's experiences, and how they trade in this foreign market.

Most of the online forex sites are run by other traders or professionals (such as brokers), who will give an insight and information about what it take to trade in the forex market.

As this market is extremely different than NYSE or NASDAQ, these sites are generally going to target those coming from those markets, for them to learn what is required to trade on that market.

Depending on the blog site and writer, information about the stocks, the companies, the foreign market in general, currency rates and currency exchange rates, and all other information about the forex market, in order for those who plan on entering the market, to learn what is required to trade in the forex market.

It is extremely different than local US markets

Since it is extremely different than local US markets, those who plan on trading in forex, should read as many forex trading blog sites and posts as possible, in order for them to learn the market and learn what it requires to trade in that market.

When choosing which forex sites to read, making sure they are professional bloggers and professional traders in forex, is of extreme importance, in order to ensure the information written in the forex blog sites is accurate.

Whether you have traded in forex in the past, or are a first time trader (or planning on becoming a first time trader), you will find that reading several blog sites prior to trading in the market, is extremely valuable for one to do, so that they can gain a basic understanding of that market and its requirements (if you really want to earn big in the market).

21

Forex Trading Chart

Forex trading charts help a trader to analyze the market trends and have become a necessity to succeed in the field of Forex trading. There are three types of charts generally used: Line charts, bar charts and the candle stick charts. This post covers various aspects related to Forex charts and some effective tips that will help you to analyze these charts.

Line charts are quite easy to understand as they consist of a single line that represents price action in time. Bar charts and candle stick charts are used to represent complex information like high and low in a given time period.

At the top of every chart details like currency pairs and time frame is mentioned. Currency pair consists of two different currencies like EUR/USD and USD/JPY.

For instance, suppose at the top of chart currency pair is mentioned as EUR/USD it means that the chart uses these two currencies as base.

Time frame also varies

Time frame also varies from chart to chart and can range from minutes to weeks. These time frames are associated with different trading styles. For instance, the scalpers use 5 minute charts while day traders utilize the 15 minute charts.

Each candle consists of a central body and an upper or lower wick. The starting point of the body represents the opening price while the end point represents the closing price.

The opening and closing price

The color of the body can be used to interpret the details related to the opening and closing price. For instance, red color is used for lower closing price while higher closing price is represented by blue or green color.

You should always remember that the charts are meant to analyze the trends and do not depict an exact information. This is because there are many other factors that affect the currency movements.

For instance, you cannot judge the impact of political factors through these charts. I hope this post helped you to learn the basics of Forex trading charts.

22

Forex Trading Courses

The use of forex trading courses are in place with several companies, in order to give first time traders or new traders experience in how to go about running their online forex account.

When choosing a company to register with, traders must find those which offer free trading courses, in order for them to gain an understanding of the foreign markets and currencies, in order for them to do well when trading.

The courses are going to help

The courses are going to help traders gain the knowledge and experience on how to properly trade, in order to maximize their potential for earning big.

There are several courses that can be chosen by traders. Whether it is to learn about the market in general, learn about the best stocks and investments, or how to learn about the currencies and exchange rates, there are many forex trading courses that can be taken by those who register with a company for a forex account.

The more information traders gain

The more information traders gain prior to starting, and the more trading courses they take prior to actually investing their own money in to stocks, the greater the chances are that they will do well when they are actually trading real money on these investment accounts.

So, no matter which Forex Company or account you choose to register with, new investors will find that taking a few trading courses prior to actually investing their own money into a stock or investment, will ensure they do not lose big on the market.

And, in fact, the more trading courses they take prior to trading, the greater the chances are that an investor is actually going to do extremely well on the market, and earn the highest returns on the investments and stock options that they are purchasing.

23

Trading Forex Online

Trading FOREX online, currency market is the place where traders can sell and buy their desired foreign currencies. This platform works entirely on computer and therefore it is possible.

A trader can place order in foreign exchange market 24 hours a day from all over the world. The market remains open five days a week. Initially, the facility of trading FOREX online was available only to institutional investors including hedge funds or investment banks. But now individual investors can also grab their part of profit with the expansion of online trading concept.

Generally, a trading platform, and often a web portal or an online application is offered by numerous reliable online brokers. Online trading account enables trader making trades and managing account using his own computer, sitting anywhere in the world.

Free Demo Account

It's strongly recommended to play with a free demo account before using your live trading account, and spend a considerable time to understand different situations, and overall FOREX trading process to develop strategy making skills.

Search for reliable local FOREX trading broker who provides facility of trading FOREX online. Any person, resident of any country can open an account with any US broker who provides services over sea.

Mostly reliable brokers provide an opportunity of opening a practice account. You must select this option as a starter. You're provided real time market stats in this practice account.

Practice Account

This practice account will help you in making decision if you're fit enough to invest in this market. Your decision depends on your learning skills, understanding of the system and your power of decision making at the right time with right choice of indicators.

Most of the reliable, highly reputable FOREX brokers have useful material on their websites. Invest some time to read them all. You'll feel most of these materials familiar to you especially if you're familiar with stock trading.

Keep learning to get maximum information about FOREX trading techniques and strategies. Try using your practice account and place some dummy orders after learning basic knowledge of this financial market.

After spending a week with your practice account, make decision to start practical account with full confidence.

24

Best Accurate Forex

Do not mortgage your home or even take out a bank loan to trade. The Use of the Best Accurate Forex Tools and Trading Signals is one thing you will need in investing nowadays.

Making your Money work is harder these days, especially that the recession almost got everybody into fearing the loss of their invested money.

However, most people still manage to grow their money with the right predictions using the best tools there are. Anybody interested in investing these days would even be glad that these forex tools are everywhere on the Internet. With simple clicks of a button, one can learn how to trade in the Forex market and get the best, accurate investment information on international currencies.

There is a wealth of information about Forex on the Internet. It only takes time and dedication from a resolute trader to know all of the basic facts, and by himself with the help of the best tools, win over his money and gain some more.

After all, the Forex is a game of probabilities, and calculated risk-taking is important in this game. A lot of people are in Forex trading because of the thrill of risk-taking and calculating the possibilities of a gaining or losing investment.

One of the perks of having good Forex tools

One of the perks of having good Forex tools is that you get the best accurate Forex trading signals. This is a good aid when it comes to your Forex trade forecasting.

Unlike other tools that only get you to trade on specific situations, accurate Forex trading signals alert you always in more ways than one. In other words, you'll be getting good trading signals at any time of the day.

For beginners, it would be a good start if you land on a Forex trading sites that have the best accurate Forex trading signals. It would give you a good lift on the real Forex trading places, and in no time you may be making good money autopilot! However, before investing, one must remember, that it is still important to look first at the site where you'll be investing your money.

Look them up first at Forex review sites, and while you are at it, search for good trading sites that have the best accurate Forex tools and trading signals.

Best accurate Forex, forex represents foreign exchange meaning, the exchange of existent currencies. A trader will purchase one currency like U.S. dollar and sell another currency called as exchange trading or forex.

Due to local and world economy fluctuations, the currency will suffer frequent value changes. So it is also easy for the traders to make profit. It is called as currency speculation and it is great option to earn money. There are plenty of advantages on trading best accurate forex.

It is the strongest market in gaining profit. The business involves with trading between two currencies, and it may take place when one currency increases, and another currency will go down if there is depreciation in the value of currency.

It is the right time to purchase so that you can sell the same currency, which you bought when it goes high at a good price.

Forex industry is a liquid market, the reason you will not be able to change your trades into cash. This is real if your currency is a big one.

The raised liquidity

The raised liquidity is useful to ensure that spreads are narrow, and the costs are equilibrated by the whole period of time.

Forex market does not have closing time, trading currencies can be performed by traders at 24 hours from Sunday to Friday. This is very easy for many people to make certain movements if the currency value changes. The important thing in the forex trading business is to be updated with the latest news. The level of liquidity of currency makes it cheaper to trade.

This is the main reason for most of the traders to purchase and sell only the big currencies. The major currencies will have a great level of liquidity; additionally, there are no commissions in major currency movements. The profits and losses are offered to the currencies difference. If you plan properly, you can easily see profits in forex trading.

25

Online Forex Trading

Online forex trading means: buying and selling of foreign currencies via online. Forex market is an international financial market where people invest in foreign currencies and make profits.

In the forex market exchange rate is the rate at which one currency is traded against another one. The increase or decrease in the exchange rate can determine whether the investor is making profit or loss. Investors who make the online trading can sit in home and make the transactions.

Online trading method

In fact, online trading method has made the forex investment a transparent one to the investors. The only motive behind any investment including forex trading is to gain positive return. People can buy one currency when its value depreciate in terms of another currency and exchange it when the value appreciates. The difference in the exchange rate between the time of buying and selling of currencies determines the level of profit. In the forex trading people often argue that they need to sit in front of computer for a long time. It is very crucial to look at even minor changes in exchange rate.

Making appropriate decisions

The market index should be carefully watched to gain profits by making appropriate decisions regarding when to make the transactions. Therefore forex trading has been treated by people as a risky investment. However they have found out a solution for enabling easy forex trading systems.

Software called forex software has been created in order to make the trade with predetermined strategies. There is no need to sit in front of the computer all the daylong to make forex trading. The forex software will work for you and you can spend your time for something else. There is forex software that offers a higher level of accuracy in the transactions in forex trading.

26

Genuine Online Trading

Genuine online trading, there are many online trading forex sites that exist in the world today but finding the genuine site can be an uphill task.

Armed with the required knowledge of the particular needs and desires that require satisfaction, one is able to secure the best online trading site that will comprehensively address their needs.

It's important that clients understand the websites' potential to fulfill their specifications, as far as online trading is concerned. What better way to secure an online trading site that provides free support, and gives the clients the required sense of security as far as their funds is concerned?

Access to the online accounts

Due to today's increasing online fraud and crimes, there must be restriction of any unauthorized access to the online accounts. A genuine system will provide an avenue, whereby the clients can easily do an in depth analysis of the current online market trends.

This is important as it will promote the client's awareness of the markets and enable them to make informed decisions. One can never assume the importance of information when they are about to make an online financial decisions that carry a significant risk factor.

Fast execution is one aspect that will improve reliability of a good trading site. There are many phone users that have integrated their banking activities to the mobile phones. Therefore, online trading has an upper hand as far as online service delivery is concerned.

Promote a sense of trust

It has a web based and mobile solution to trading. The pages should also be downloadable. Genuine online trading should also be based on the maxim effective, one-on-one training is offered to those willing to venture into online trading.

This will improve the client's understanding of the online trading activities and improve their perception of the same. Genuine trading should also be guided by necessary regulations that will govern the online operations and protect clients from fraudsters. This will not only guard the clients' online accounts but also promote a sense of trust in online trading.

27

Forex Trading News

The Forex trading news is by far one of the largest and also the most liquid financial markets in the world, due to its complexity and other several advantages.

It's uniqueness of being open 24/7 for all traders is a very convenient fact; therefore there are an increased number of stock exchange traders nowadays that are starting to use a Forex platform.

The main benefits and advantages that made Forex trading become so popular in our modern world are:

A 24/7 Market:

A 24/7 Market: since this market can be accessed worldwide, not just in a specific country, the trading is continuous, day and night. Usually, the trading starts right when the market opens on Sunday evening in Australia and ends right after the market in New York has closed on Friday night.

High Liquidity market: this is probably one of the greatest advantages of Forex. The liquidity is crucial today, as it represents the ability for a specific asset to be converted easily and very quickly into cash, without an additional price discount or tax. With the Forex trading news, you trade with currency, which allows you to move very large amounts of money into various foreign currencies with a minimal price movement tax.

Leverage:

Leverage: another great advantage of Forex trading is that it allows for a high leverage rate. This means you can trade in the market with additional money than actually are in that moment in your account.

For example, if you trade at a rate of 20:1 leverage, that means you could trade exactly $20 on the market for every $1 that you have in your account. A very advantageous thing, in my opinion, as you can control a large trade of $20,000 with only $1000 of your capital.

A High Profit: this is in the end the goal of every trader that uses the Forex trading platform.

The good thing about this is the trader determines this beforehand and they can choose which news report would be useful or dangerous in trading.

28

Online Trading Tools

Online trading tools, adopting them in trading is an essential move for traders, however, with the abundance of many trading tools, it is wise to consider tried and tested ones, and the ones which really suits your trading style. For you to be guided in choosing your tool, here is a short discussion of them.

Trading assistance tools

These tools comprises of signal software, Meta trader, trend analyzer, and strategy builder. Although, each of these assistance tools has their own unique features, their main function is to give you alerts when it is time to start trading and other important signals. Alerts are very important if you are a busy person and tend to forget. Assistance tools are handy because they can send signals to any part of the earth. It also helps in the analysis of trends and other information presented in the chart.

Trading Software and Charts

Under this category are micro lots, forex training forex charts, forex websites, forex tools, and forex API tools. Software and charts are also an important online trading tool since both provides you with features capable of analyzing trends, allowing you to make your own algorithms, and to create multiple positions in just a single click.

Permits investors to connect

Market Tracking

This includes Market tracking that permits investors to connect directly to the market vendors. Currency converter that can convert more than fifty separate currencies giving the trader the

Convenience to promptly see currency rates is also another market tracking tool. The forex calculators which provide you a rough estimate of exchange rate are also an essential market tracking tool.

Whichever tool you choose to use, it is always safe to learn it well as if the trading tool is your masterpiece. Once you master how to use your tool, it becomes your best friend in your trading stardom.

29

Forex Exchange

Forex Exchange means foreign currency. Currency of one country is the foreign currency of another country. In the international financial market, currencies of various countries are being traded by the investors.

Again, there are many investors who invest millions of dollars in the forex exchange market and earn huge profits even with a small change in the currency value. This is how the exchange works and what makes the basis for making profit in the forex market.

Again, a currency can either appreciate or depreciate its value in terms of another currency due to its demand and supply conditions. When there is higher demand for a particular currency then its value tend to increase and vice versa.

There is inverse relationship

On the other hand, there is inverse relationship between supply of a currency and its value. The basis for making profit or loss is the changes in the value of currencies in terms of another currency.

Let us analysis how the profit can be measured with the help of an example. Suppose one Dollar is equal to 1.5 pound in international market and further if the value of dollar increases in terms of pound then one Dollar can fetch more than 1.5 pound.

The difference will be the rate of profit to the investor. This does not mean that investment will always fetch profits. It depends on whether the currency that you invested would appreciate or depreciate its value in terms of another one.

Many people invest in forex market

There are many people who invest in forex market working from home, making transactions online. This has made the investment options easier in the financial market.

The only thing that investors should take care of is to calculate the rate of change in the value of the currencies, and make proper decisions regarding when to make the transaction, so that the profit can be assured.

30

Forex Trading Demo

Whether you use trading bots, or whether you visit trading sites which can give you a basic forex trading demo, there are several methods to learn about the forex market, and how to trade in it. here are many sites for those who are just entering the forex market can turn to, in order to get a free demo on how to trade, when to trade, what stocks to consider, and various other pieces of information which can be learned by watching these online demo videos. Depending on the sites you visit, and depending on the information a trader seeks, there are many videos which can be watched.

When choosing the forex demo videos to watch, traders must consider the site, it's content, and whether or not it is a reliable place to be getting information from.

There are hundreds of free sites

There are hundreds of free sites on the web which teach traders several tips and techniques on the forex market via videos; but, as a trader, taking the time to get more information about those sites, and making sure they are reliable and accurate informational sources, is also something the trader has to consider when they are entering the forex market, to ensure they are receiving accurate information from the sites and the videos they have watched.

Most of the information you get online is accurate, and most site hosts tend to have a fair amount of knowledge about the forex market. But, just to be on the safe side, for those who have never traded on the forex market, and want to get information and tips about certain investments they are considering, will find that watching various forex videos will help them determine which ones are accurate, and which ones they should avoid.

31

Forex Trading Indicators

A FOREX trader should learn FOREX trading indicators if they want to become a successful investor in this financial market. There're several different indicators to select by a trader.

Though applying these indicators doesn't guarantee profit since foreign currency exchange market is basically a speculative venture.

But applying the right indicator can minimize your losses and make good returns on your investment. Therefore learning all available indicators is a key to greatly enhance your chances.

The leading indicators

First, you should familiarize yourself with available types of indicators before started applying them. All available indicators in the FOREX trading market are covered in two types: (1) The leading indicators (2) The lagging indicators.

The leading indicators are used to get indication about a buy signal before reversal or new trend appears. On the other hand, a lagging indicator is used by a FOREX trader to get indication after the trend changes.

Oscillators, is another term/name which is used for the leading indicators. These indicators include tools, such as the Ultimate Oscillator and the MACD (Moving Average Convergence Divergence). The tools like Bollinger Bands and the Moving Averages are included in the lagging indicators, also identified as momentum oscillators.

Developing a trading plan

Developing a trading plan is truly essential for FOREX traders because it keeps them consistent in their trading. It also helps in avoiding irrational decisions which are likely to make occasionally in different situations including market sentiments and emotions, but should be made based on fundamentals. The type of the market is vital to consider before making a good trading plan, because indicators provide different results based on the market type.

Select the best suitable FOREX trading indicator based on the market type. A practice account can be an asset to learn different market types and different indicators.

The leading indicators are considered good to start because they inform before a trend change occurs. But wide fluctuations in the FOREX market make them highly inaccurate sometimes. These types of markets where wide fluctuations are routine matters, the lagging indicators should be applied.

Forex Trading Tutorial

Forex trading tutorial, to become a profitable forex trader you need to learn from a high-quality forex trading tutorial, which can be pleasurable and an experience for you. Success in forex trading is not an easier task, so you got to pay for a best forex trading training from valued and eligible sources.

Be sure to know about the sources, if you are searching it on the Internet, as many internet traders tries to make good money from the world of forex. Honestly, you will find the best training from a professional marketer, who knows how and what it is to be successful in forex trading.

A fruitful strategy

When you have learned about forex marketing, don't ever try to deal real money unless a constant amount of profit is grabbed from a demo trading account. A fruitful strategy will be established after you get a high quality of training from a skilled marketer.

Only think making deal with real money when you will be able to implement this strategy gainful with a sample/demo account. First of all you need to have a valuable and respectful source for your training.

Many websites are offering you a forex training tutorials, but sadly only a little of them are genuine. Do make some research before you go. The sites providing you free tutorials are likely to be genuine; on the other hand sites which don't provide free tutorials are just scams. So away from them!

Training from a professional

It's totally on you, whether you take it easily or with difficulties, but gaining training from a qualified trader can definitely change the way of your learning. The best way to learn forex trading is to obtain the training from a professional.

A skilled trainer can help you avoid losing a handsome amount of dollars, which so many marketers struggle to do after years of trial. Just don't look at offers that might seem impressive, they will just frustrate you in the end. The forex tutorial can keep the technical part of forex trading ease but efficient, so just use it!

33

Forex Trading Strategy

Forex traders who do not have the effective forex trading strategy find the forex market frustrating. To avoid the same fate, you need to be armed with strategies to survive the tricky world of forex business.

Although, earnings from short positions are lesser than the long positions, opting for them is a better choice. This is because the forex market is unstable in which it changes from time to time without you noticing the changes if you are not attentive.

Changes are crucial to pay attention to because it affects your earnings. Maintaining at least 2 or 3 short positions allows you to stay focused and can trade effectively. In addition, you may earn decent profits just the same with short positions if earnings are added altogether.

For example, in a 10 short positions earning .002 pips if summed up may give you total earnings of .02 which is still a good gain. If this is sustained occasionally, it becomes a better strategy to make your account fat. To some, doing it slowly but surely is a reliable strategy.

Protecting Your Investment

Protecting your investment is also another forex trading strategy. One way of shielding your money is to do hedging, strategy where the trader stays put on both sides of the currency pairs. The trader invests on both sides to counter act the effect of the other.

What Happens Now?

In using this strategy, no matter what happens with the Investment, the profit is get-even because there is no lose and a win. If for instance, one pair of your chosen currency is predicted to make it strong but risky enough to suck your investment, staying on the other pair may counter such negative effect. Hedging is however employed by seasoned forex traders because they are comfortable with it. Starters are advised not to try it if they are not yet accustomed with how it is done.

34

Best Forex Trading

If you are venturing to join the pool of successful forex traders, here is the best forex trading techniques.

You may adopt, to eventually hurdle the ins and outs of this business.

First, is to have a schedule at hand. This should contain the list of the hours you are able to do the trading. Attempt to join in the times of the day where you can really make the deal. At best, select your most comfortable schedule where nobody could disturb you.

Trading is a business that needs concentration so that outside interruptions should be avoided. Once you are disrupted, you might lose your precious chance of making it big on certain trading.

Activities in forex trading change in seconds or minutes which requires the concentration of the trader.

To some traders, they find the best forex trading in listening to news cast about trading. This is actually the secret of successful traders since they are abreast of all the news and changes within the business for them to make changes in their trading style.

News serves as the guide for traders if it suits them best to trade for the day or not.

Another trading technique

Another trading technique is for the trader to have enough investment. Trading is like any other business that needs to have a sustainable investment. This is if you want to stay longer in your trade.

It does not mean, you have to have thousands or millions in your account but at least a few hundreds. Make sure not to put all your money in a single trade because you might lose it all at once and you are finish.

The strategy is to do it bit by bit until you become a pro. As a beginner, you have to be satisfied with small pips in your account.

Lastly, you should know how to execute the stop loss. A trader who is equipped with this technique is for sure a winner. Stop loss is merely stopping trading when you reached your desired earning for the day.

Traders who are greedy to continuously trading find it a mistake to do so. They may lose all their earnings for the day including their investment. This makes it wise to know when to stop loss.

35

Forex Trading Guide

Forex Trading Guide, Traders are provided an opportunity to earn massive income at once by the Foreign Exchange market, which isn't seen across the globe in any other financial market.

More than $4 trillion is traded per day in this market, and if you're familiar with how to trade in the FOREX market, you can grab you share as well. A firm grasp of FOREX trading basics is a must to be successful in this market. This FOREX trading guide will try to teach you the way to success.

To sell and buy currencies

In this market, traders get opportunity to sell and buy currencies, two simultaneously: the quote currency and the base currency. You'll always see two currencies at the FOREX quotes listed together.

The quote currency will be seen following the base currency in the list. Placing a buy order means that the base currency is being purchased and the quote currency is being sold. You hope that the value of the base currency will increase against the quote currency.

The trader has only one objective i.e. to generate a profit. Exchange rate fluctuations between traded countries are the only way that allow trader to earn profit.

A trader can get involved in a few different types of trades in this market.

The market order

The market order can be placed in short or long position. It means that any currency pair can be sold or purchased immediately at the market price. A limit order can also be placed in the FOREX trading market with specified minimum or maximum price, which a trader wants to set for the transaction.

Another term in this trading market is stop order. This type of order is placed in foreign currency exchange market to close out an order only, when the currency price reaches a preset certain point. There is a great deal of risk involved in FOREX market. Therefore, learning or understanding legitimate trading strategy of this market is really important.

36

How to trade

How to Trade In Forex Market, there are many people wondering about how others are making investments in the forex market. They are very curious to know trading in the foreign exchange market. There are many ways regarding trading in the forex market.

The optimum strategy that you follow to make the transactions can make you a higher level of return. Therefore, it is quite necessary to understand trading in the forex market in order to accrue profits.

Forex market various

It is worth knowing what actually happens in the forex market. In the forex market various currencies are being traded by the investors. They will buy one currency by analyzing its value in terms of another currency and will sell it by calculating the changes in exchange rate.

It is true that various currencies have different values in the international financial market. The values here imply the value of one currency in terms of another currency. In other words, it means how much currency can be bought by spending a particular amount of another currency.

Therefore, investors will buy a particular currency when it has lower value in terms of another currency and will sell it according to the increase in exchange rate.

There are online methods

There are online methods available to make the transactions in forex market. You can run your business from home and make trade in the financial market. You should always take a good decision regarding when to buy and when to sell a particular currency.

It is worth knowing the past exchange rates between two currencies before making a decision regarding your investment. Even a small change in the exchange rate can make you a big gain or loss depending upon the total amount of your investment. There are many investors who earn higher level of profits by investing millions of dollars in the forex market.

37

Auto Forex Trading System

The Consistent Profits with Auto Forex Trading, traders are looking for a trading system that they can use to trade with. The thought of having trades entered and exited automatically is very good thought.

This is especially true when the trades being made are profitable. It is a very good feeling to wake up to money in your Forex account without having to do anything, while you know other traders have been up for a few hours!

When you heard about auto Forex trading, the first thing that enters you mind is automatic trading software or Forex robot. Well, there are still other kinds of automated system that is designed to take only half of your work while leaving you in full control of the whole trading process.

This system is called Forex trading signals. It has the ability to monitor and analyze the direction of the market, and point out the perfect opportunity to enter the market, and gain great benefits and advantages.

So if you're going to be switching over to auto Forex trading, then what options do you have? Well, there are programs that you can buy called "Forex robots."

These programs automatically enter and exit trades for you with the intention of turning a profit. You can leave one of these Forex robots on all day long, and do as you please while it trades the Forex market for you.

A lot of Forex traders eventually do decide to make the switch to an auto Forex trading system, or "Forex robot", but then there is the problem of deciding which one to use.

Obviously, we all would like to use the one that is going to make us the most money, but which one is that? I'll let you know later on in this article which one is the best selling, and also the one that is the most profitable, but how do we know that it's the best?

When looking for a Forex Robot

When looking for a Forex robot, we need to find one that the owner does not hide things about it. Screenshots of the robot trading live accounts are always a good thing. Another thing to look for is the reviews from other traders. You can always look around on Forex forums for reviews from actual traders.

Since auto Forex trading has different kinds and features, you also need to choose not only for the best but for a system that goes along with your trading style and personality.

You should have to evaluate these systems, know their functions as well as their disadvantages, and pick for what you think will bring good fortunes on your trade. The good trader never gets tired of searching for options. Now, that's how patience and endurance come in the picture.

Advantages and Disadvantages of Half Automated System:

With this type of automated trading system, you have the full authority to make every decision and the one that runs the whole trading process. The system is only the one responsible in tracking for profitable signals and opportunities as well as evaluating the market condition.

On the other hand, you can choose when to enter the market and is free to choose from different trading options you wish to use.

The only disadvantage so far with this system is you might actually fail to recognize trading signal that could bring good profits, or because you lack of proper guidance, *you might actually ignore great opportunities.*

Advantages and Disadvantages of Full Automated System: The major advantage of this system is its ability to run the whole trading process by itself even without the interaction of the trader.

Automated Software

With automated software, all executions and commands of the traders are programmed in the computer and it is the one doing all the complicated jobs for 24 hours during trading days.

What's more interesting with this system is your trade may be in the hands of the technology, but, it will still run according to your plans and trading style.

On the other hand, this type of automated system will surely knock your wallet out. Subscribing in a VPS service will cost you much money, not to mention the risk you are taking by not getting personally involved with your own trade.

38

Easy Forex

Learn easy Forex Trading Strategies before You enter in to forex. The forex trading strategies for new traders is the use of currency monitoring to expect market movements and currency changes.

There are two various methods are used by the experienced traders to check about currency and these analysis are technical and fundamental analysis.

Technical analysis is the cost of currency pairs and it is used to assist and to know about the market trends and calculate the cost volatility of the currency to identify the trading indicators.

Fundamental analysis consists on looking outside and state factors which can impact the currency value like stability of existing political condition, unemployment rate, of the country that affect the currency value.

Both types of analysis are important

Both types of analysis are important and help the new traders because these analyses are not difficult and the trading indicators are normally clear. Some may prefer to use technical, and some may like to use fundamental analysis in their forex trading market.

This will be making them more successful after making a trail in the demo account. Day trading is the famous easy forex trading strategy and it is right choice for the beginners.

By following this strategy, the new trader will not hold trading position, but they will purchase at the day time and leave all the positions at the end of the same day.

The length of time you hold the position will be your high risk on losing the trade. It helps the beginners to make large amount of little trades on the single day without involving in the great risk with the positions they hold.

The costs of the currency are frequently changes

The costs of the currency are frequently changes on the day and the traders have to take advantage of using the fluctuations in the currency pairs to become profitable in the business.

This day trading is ideal option for new traders and experienced traders in the easy forex business. For every new trader, it is important to educate themselves before entering into the forex market. You can easily learn online and there are plenty of resources are available to offer free forex education, possibly the highest leverage in the industry. Unfortunately, all of these offers are not available to US residents.

39

Forex Trading Forex

Forex trading forex, Forex represents foreign exchange meaning, the exchange of existent currencies. A trader will purchase one currency like U.S. dollar and sell another currency called as exchange trading or forex.

Due to local and world economy fluctuations, the currency will suffer frequent value changes. So it is also easy for the traders to make profit. It is called as currency speculation and it is great option to earn money.

There are plenty of advantages on trading forex. It is the strongest market in gaining profit. The business involves with trading between two currencies and it may take place when one currency increases and another currency will go down if there is depreciation in the value of currency.

It is the right time to purchase so that you can sell the same currency which you bought when it goes high at a good price. Forex trading forex industry is liquid market, the reason you will not be able to change your trades in to cash.

This is real if your currency is big one. The raised liquidity is useful to ensure that spreads are narrow and the costs are equilibrated by the whole period of time.

24 hours from Sunday to Friday

Forex trading forex market does not have closing time, trading currencies can be performed by traders at 24 hours from Sunday to Friday. This is very easy for many people to make certain movements if the currency value changes.

The important thing in the forex trading business is to be updated with the latest news. The level of liquidity of currency makes cheaper to trade.

This is main reason for most of the traders to purchase and sell only the big currencies. The major currencies will have great level of liquidity; additionally there are no commissions in major currency movements.

The profits and losses are offered to the currencies difference. If you plan properly, you can easily see profits in forex trading. Just you should follow some tips to become successful in forex market.

First educate yourself; you should know what is involves with the market analysis and checking the aspects that affect the currency value.

Forex Trading Software

You must know nation economic policies and political circumstances affect the currency. It is a money market and so it is necessary to take a quick decision when needed. Along with this ability, you should have good plan and forex strategy.

Forex trading relates with high risk, so before entering in to the forex field, you should check whether you can handle the various situation that come while trading in the forex market. You should be prepared to lose your money while trading forex.

Having good forex trading software will help you to prevent loss. But you have to be very careful on choosing the software for your trading purposes. You should make sure whether the software offers all kinds of protection of your information.

It is also good to have an effective forex broker along with you in the time to advise you to make best movements in the forex trading. It is also easy for you to make profits in the best way.

40

Forex Trading Forum

There are a number of Forex trading forums available online, where different members discuss the latest happenings related to financial market. These forums can be really helpful as you can learn from the experiences of other traders.

However, since a number of members are present on such forums you may get conflicting information. Thus you need to be careful while using the forums. This post contains various useful tips that will guide you to make the maximum of the forums.

Trading forums contain members

The trading forums contain members with different level of expertise regarding financial market. At such, it is not necessary that every post or information provided in the forum is true.

Therefore, do not take any information or tip for granted. You should first test the strategy on a demo trading account. If you see some good results, you can try the same strategy with the real account.

Understand the logic

You should try to understand the logic behind any prediction or statement. Later when you have gained some experience, you would be able to filter good and useful information from the Forex trading forums. Another benefit of these forums is that you can ask for suggestions from other members after giving a brief outline of your strategy.

There are a number of tools available on the trading forums that can prove to be helpful. There are charts available that can help you to understand trends and patterns in the market. You should try to correlate the changes in the trends with the possible causes.

You can also find guided tours on these forums that are specially meant for the beginners. Again you will find a forecast and news section that can help you to plan your strategies in a better way. I hope these tips will help you to use forums efficiently.

41

Forex Trading Scams

Forex trading scams, the forex market ranks among the largest trading markets in the world, but as the popularity of forex trading continues to grow; forex trading scams are as well popping up by the day. Newbie forex traders with little experiences are usually the target for online forex scammers, who typically use the guise of online forex trading to scam the unsuspecting victims of their hard earned cash.

This article will share with you several signals for online scams, so you can avoid falling victims to the traps of these scammers.

Many types of scams

Popular forex scams

There are many types of scams on the internet today, and most of them not only look very legitimate at first glance, but they are also very compelling.

Signal sellers

Companies promising their customers information on the type of trades to make on a specific day are popping up by the day. Such companies typically charge their customers a fee per week, or per month to "update" them regularly, but in essence, they hardly improve their trading. If someone had a magic formula to the forex trading market, would he/she be selling it out for a few hundred dollars? Of course he/she would want to keep it a secret.

Guaranteed investment funds

There has also been a proliferation of guaranteed High Yield Investment Programs, or HYIPs, that promise unreasonable, guaranteed rate of return (as high as 12%) on investors' capital. As with any trading market, forex market cannot offer guaranteed interest rates and this is the first forex trading scam signal to watch out for. If anything, it doesn't sound economically logical that a single trader can consistently make a profit of 12% per day as that would destabilize the world's economy in a matter of days if not months.

What most of these HYIP companies essentially do is to use new investor's money to pay older investors and so on. In the event that no more investors are enrolling, the companies shut down and run away with all the cash remaining in their hands.

Plenty of software online

Magic software

There is plenty of software online that promise to figure out the best moves for the traders. Do a simple Google search and you will come across hundreds, if not thousands of them retailing for as high as $5,000.

Most of these will do nothing than just provide you with simple information that you can as well find online for free.

In conclusion, the old adage, if it is too good to be true think twice holds true for the forex trading market. Follow your instincts and engage the sixth sense to avoid falling for the forex trading scams that many people have fallen into. Also, remember that forex trading is risky and nobody with good intentions would try to convince you otherwise.

42

Learn Forex Trading

Learn Forex Trading, are you a beginner but interested in forex trading? Here is how you can beat the forex world. The initial step to learn-forex-trading is to teach you the basics of forex. The old saying "knowledge is power" applies in this kind of online business.

Anybody going into trading not equipped with enough knowledge is likely to lose his investment in a short period of time. For you not be among those losers, you need to learn some commonly used terms in the business. This is to make you comfortable with those words to be able to apply them as it is needed.

Trainings are also very important

Trainings are also very important for novice traders to learn-forex-trading. One way of training yourself is to try playing on free trading sites.

Fortunately enough, there are many online trading sites giving free trials to prospect traders.

You just open an account with them and you are ready for the trial. The demo account will help you create some plans or strategies to be able to compete with the experienced traders if you will be in the real arena of trading. Training should not stop there but rather continuous. Even in the event you become experienced traders, there is still a need to update yourself of the new tools and other trends in trading.

To learn forex trading

Finally, to learn-forex-trading is to wisely choose the currency you are expecting to trade and the right time of the day to trade. Although, there are many currency pairs to choose from, the right choice is very important in trading if earning big bucks is to be considered.

Usually, the most commonly traded currency pairs are USD/EUR and USD/AUD because they are traded during the busiest trading time of the day which means the pairs kick more earnings than the exotic currency pairs. Apart from this, you need to be available during the session you chose to participate. You might lose the critical time where you are supposed to have the big break in you trading.

43

Learn Trading Online

Learn Trading Online; even if thousands of people are daily jumping into the online trading community, still then the most important question is how to learn trading?

There are so many companies offering to provide the knowledge to carry out online trading that it has become quite difficult to choose one. With the abundance of information available, only the right decisions at the right time and the right online trading courses can assist in making some cash out of this business.

Number of companies offering

There are a large number of companies offering to teach trading online. One can get these courses in document formats, audio or video formats. As a beginner, you can take the information to build a solid platform.

For the intermediate and the experts, these courses may help elevate you to a higher level. The key point would be to search for the flaw in the trading strategy you are following and search for a course that can help improve upon the area.

Before taking a course to learn trading, one should take a look at the time span of the course. Every person has a different speed of capturing information. Courses may span from weeks to years all together.

The willingness to learn

It all depends upon the willingness to learn, the amount of time you have and the availability of the course. The cost is also an important factor because it may vary from being free to thousands of dollars. The value of any course cannot be known until you can consult with a person who has already taken the course.

The final and the most important thing in the process to learn trading online, is the application part. First open a demo online trading account as well as a live one if you want to avoid the hassles of setting it up one later.

One of the best would be a forex trading company. Then if you are happy with the demo trades, you can start to trade with your live account and make some good cash.

44

Online Currency Trading

Online Currency Trading, currency trading is a major source of investment in the international financial market. There are lots of investors who make the gains by engaging in the currency trading.

As the Information technology has improved in the past decades to a very extend people are being attracted to the online currency trading. You can engage in trading in currencies of various countries by looking at your computer monitor. All the transactions will be made via online and the money can be transacted to your bank accounts online itself.

Demand for foreign currencies

Currency trading is happening for most of the currencies in the world. As no country is self sufficient in resources each country is engaged in import and exports of goods and services. This has created a demand for foreign currencies with greater economic interdependence among countries.

The value of a currency is decided by its demand and supply. Due to the variations in these market forces the value of a currency keep on changing with respect to another currency. As trade between two currencies occurs there will be a rate what we call exchange rate that moves up or down.

When the exchange rate lowers you can buy the currency and sell it when the exchange rate with the same currency increases. In other words these are called depreciation or appreciation of currencies.

One of the great benefits

One of the great benefits of online trading is that you can see the fluctuations in the exchange rate live on your computer screen. It will help you make a proper decision regarding when to make the transactions and make profit.

The only thing needed is you have to sit in front of the computer looking at even the minor changes in the exchange rate. However, there automatic trading systems in the market which can enable you to make transactions for you with predetermined strategies.

45

Managed Forex Trading

Managed Forex Trading, even if people jump into the online trading business for great returns, but trading currency on your own is a highly difficult, time consuming and frustrating task.

There are many traders who love to do online trading, but due to the lack of time to learn the currency market and to track the investments, make this task highly difficult.

Here the professional trading companies come to the rescue. These companies have people who are seated to study the market 365 days a year. They are hired to study every change in the currency levels with passing by time.

A managed forex account

This is something that a normal trader cannot do. The help of these highly qualified traders can be taken with the help of a managed account.

A managed forex account is an individual trading account that is managed with thousands of other managed trading accounts and is used upon as some percentage of the whole trade. Any profit or loss is divided equally among all the account holders.

The professional trader

The professional trader can't directly access your funds until properly authorized. The investor retains the full control on the account throughout and the trader is only allowed a limited access to the account with a power of attorney which can be invoked anytime. This does provide greater security to the account and allows you to have control over it.

The traders use software to manage all the account and any profit or loss incurred is divided equally in between all the accounts that participated in the trade.

Even if a managed forex trading account do not remove the risk present in currency trading, but it also gives higher returns and also allows to follow a trader who is experienced in this field. Even if it is a great way, but finding an efficient broker who can handle such type of trading can be the most challenging task.

46

Online Trading Broker

Online Trading Broker, Internet has given all the resources for individual trader to perform trading but one basic rule still applies: Trader needs a broker so he can perform trading better. Choosing the right broker can indeed become a headache to beginner trader like you. Here are several things that you need to consider when you choose trading broker. For Security you must choose a legitimate broker. Do not ever hand over your hard-earned money before checking the legitimacy of the broker. Checking the legitimacy of a broker is not difficult.

Member of Regulatory Agency

Legit broker always becomes a member of Regulatory Agency in its region. If not listed as a member of Regulatory Agency, the broker is a scam. Transaction Cost Every single trade that you make is subject to transaction cost so searching for broker with low transaction cost is mandatory.

However, security should not be sacrificed only to get low transaction cost. Good balance between security and low transaction cost is better.

Deposit and Withdrawal, the broker needs to give assurance that deposit and withdrawal processes are fast and easy. The money in your account is yours so you have full right to withdraw the money at any time.

Normal market conditions

Your broker only helps you to facilitate trading and he does not have right to hold your money. Trading Platform Once you choose to trade with a broker, it means you trade using the broker's trading platform. You need to ensure that the trading platform is stable and user friendly.

The trading platform should also give all tools and data that you need to support your trading. Execution Under normal market conditions, it is mandatory for broker to suggest you in the best possible price for every trade. Broker's suggestion is vital to win the trade.

Customer Service, although broker knows more about trading than trader, broker is not perfect. Good broker always provides good customer support whenever problem arises. Reviews from other traders are also helpful to determine the credibility of online trading broker.

47

Auto Forex Traders

Auto Forex traders are different from mechanical traders in that their trading involves no decision making or human involvement. Traders rely on either forex robots or other forms of automated expert advisors, or EAs for short. There are a number of advantages that these traders have over those who rely on mechanical systems.

First, traders require users to install an automatic trading system only. Trading decisions will be made by the automated program according to developer's settings and trader's customized settings.

This means that these traders are spared from going through agonizing forex trading lessons. On their part, mechanical traders have to go through rigorous forex training.

Unfortunately, even after their training, the so called mechanical traders still lose money. It is thus wise to take advantage of automated systems and make money from the lucrative forex market. Another benefit associated with it is that systems can be back-tested. It is possible to test the effectiveness of a system before putting it into use.

Additionally, the systems come with at least 60 day money-back guarantee. This means that users can always return the product if they feel that it is not meeting their expectations. It is a fact that auto forex traders make big money from the forex market.

New Auto Traders

New auto traders, however, should not go for auto trading systems and expect to become rich overnight. Forex trading is not a get rich quick scheme. In order to make the best from an auto trading system, a trader may need to consider two main factors.

First, an automated system must be customized in such a way that it can manage traders' capital effectively. This means that the auto system must only risk a small percentage of the trader's capital per every trade.

Secondly, an excellence system must re-invest capital. Trader's capital in this case will be compounded after every trade.

48

Forex Trading Tips

Forex Trading Tips, similar to any other businesses, forex trading is not without risks. With this, a trader should be open to forex trading tips that he/she may encounter. Here are a few of them.

One is to have a simple trading style. This is to avoid confusion on your part as a trader. Simplicity is not only beauty but it may lead to money as well. This concept should be followed even if you opt to use software.

Software made simply

Software made simply with not many features in it makes your trading simple too. Most often, traders using complicated software lose their money quicker than they could earn because they concentrate more on the features of the software rather than having the attention on the actual trading.

This is usually the common mistakes of traders which should be avoided. If you make your own trading chart, make it simple as well as long as you have the most important features. In addition, you should not be intimidated with traders using the complicated styles and follow what they do. Setting your own style is a winning decision since you may discover your own way of earning.

Common mistakes of traders

Having a broker is also another trading tip to consider. Brokers play a role in making a trader successful. List some of the brokers you feel suits your needs and take the chance to participate on the free services they offer you.

This is also a test, if they are really helpful to their traders. Give extra time to check their backgrounds too. Look for reviews online however you should have an open mind if you read reviews. One negative review should not be a basis for you to terminate a broker from your list, but do more in depth research on them. You may find forums also helpful.

Exit intelligently, that is to make a trade you feel you are a winner. Do not equate forex trading with gambling where you may frustrate yourself leaving the gambling den penniless.

49

Forex Trading Education

Prior to entering this complex foreign market, traders will find that getting the proper forex trading education and training strategies will greatly benefit them in the market, and will improve their chances for success in the market.

There are several companies online, or individual traders who have become "experts" in forex that offer online seminars or live seminars that offer education and training for one to learn what is required to do well in the forex market.

Type of training

Depending on the type of training one seeks, they can take courses in learning what currency to buy into, learning the currency exchange rates and what affects them, can learn when to trade or buy, or several other topics can be chosen, depending on the education course that the student is planning on attending or registering for, prior to entering the market.

Although, it is not required that an individual take courses, if they are new to forex, and if they are new to stock trading in general, it is highly advisable for them to consider one of these courses.

When choosing the forex trading education course, the individual has to make sure that it is a reputable online site or trader offering the seminar, and they must try to find testimonials or reviews about the success others have had after taking these courses.

Education and training courses

The greater the ratings, and the more highly rated an instructor is for the seminar, the greater the chances that they are going to be a great aid for those who are looking to learn how to trade in forex. There are several education and training courses one can consider, choosing the right ones, and the most reputable ones, will ensure the greatest success when trading in the market.

50

Forex Trading Seminar

Forex trading seminars are becoming increasingly popular as more and more people attempt to make money on the foreign exchange market. The foreign exchange market used to be reserved for financial professionals, but is now open to amateurs as well as professionals.

Working with the foreign exchange market can be very difficult. That is why a plethora of books and tapes are available on the subject. The internet is also a wonderful source of material on trading currencies on the foreign exchange market. There are a great number of websites that cover currency trading in great depth and are updated frequently.

The best way to learn

However, seminars are the best way to learn about forex trading. In a seminar you have the opportunity to listen to well-crafted, live presentations given by currency trading experts. No other source of information can come close to offering the cutting edge detail a well run seminar provides.

The best way to find a forex seminar is to browse online for forex trading seminar advertisements.

Forex seminars are becoming more and more popular; consequently, it is almost guaranteed that you will find a seminar online.

Finding a good seminar online

If you are having difficulty finding a good seminar online, then you should consider contacting the authors of some of your favorite currency trading books and seeing if they are planning on holding seminars anytime soon.

A number of famous forex trading authors hold large seminars every year. If you contact enough authors, you are almost certain to hit upon at least one that holds annual seminars.

Of course, it is important to mention that finding forex seminars is only the beginning. Once you have located one, it is important to prepare yourself properly for the experience. Many of these seminars are pricey, and it would behoove you to bring all the note taking materials you can so that you can derive as much as possible from the experience.

51

Forex Trading Platforms

Forex trading platforms brought modernization in the arena of forex trading in which the pencil and paper becomes second tools. Platform became a trend for traders to do their forex business because they find it convenient to earn big bucks in a shorter time. To be successful with it though, the user has to sign up for an online account with a broker. The best thing with brokers is they do not only provide trading tools but trains their prospect users as well with their virtual cash for practice purposes.

Practice provides the trader

Practice provides the trader the opportunity to accustom himself with the features of the platform and learn the mechanics of it. As the user plays with the platform, his trading skills are polished.

Apart from this, the trader will be able to try his strategies if it is compatible with the platform. Using platform is all about suitability to the needs of the trader, so that it is a necessity to try it before it is installed on your computer.

Traders expect to find important data in the forex trading which are commonly found in real trading. The real time is shown when the user practices as if he is engaged in the real trading.

The feeling of real trader

This is to give the user the feeling of real trader. The actual cash involved is also revealed as the trader buys and sell currencies. For instance, if the trader starts with $ 50, such amount is displayed. The money expected to be gained and the amounts to lose are also shown in the platform.

Other data such as the balance available in the account and the balance expected to use in trading is readily displayed as well. Although, these are normally found in a platform, not all forex trading platforms are equipped with it. There are some platforms which do not contained some of the features mentioned while there are platforms with complete features. This makes trials important.

52

Online Trading Scams

Online trading scams has become of age in recent times and it is not hard to see the reason why this is so; while traditionally, a trader had to place orders with their brokers by way of a phone call, who would then feed the request into their systems manually for linkage with trading floors and stock exchanges, the advent of the internet has made things a whole lot easier.

Investors can now make real time orders online and even trade with other traders directly. Online brokers also charge relatively lower fees to their clients compared to offline brokers and this has made online trading a particularly attractive option for newbie traders.

Unfortunately, online scams have grown at a staggering pace. The new inexperienced traders are often gullible and scam artists often target them to swindle their money away.

For that reason, it is advisable to exercise prudence while choosing your online trading platforms and brokers. No matter how legitimate and appealing an online trading ad is, you should take the time to look around for reviews of the same.

Many unsuspecting individuals

You will specifically want to verify that the broker is licensed within the state of province in which their jurisdiction falls. That way you will be able to avoid online trading scams that many unsuspecting individuals become victims of.

Among the most common online trading scams are ponzi schemes whereby capital injected by new traders is used to pay "yesterday's" investors. And when the line of new investors fade away, the company pulls out and runs away with the investors' cash remaining in their coffers.

If you see an investing company offering you a guaranteed return on your capital, be especially cautious before engaging with them as high chances are that you will end up losing your cash.

There are also a number of online scams that out-rightly defraud unsuspecting investors of their hard earned dollars. Such companies promise the investors thousands of dollars in a short span of time, typically a few weeks or months, with an initial investment of a few thousand dollars, say $5,000. In essence however, the money is not invested in any online trading scheme but is swindled away.

There is also an increasing number of magic forex trading software retailing online that supposedly provide you with information on the moves to make at a given time.

Be particularly skeptical

Most of them if not all don't deliver on their promises and in any case, you should be particularly skeptical of automated online forex trading software products.

There are also online trading scams that take the shape of false advertising and for that reason the importance of looking for online opinions and reviews about any online trading platform or opportunity before engaging in it cannot be overemphasized.

Lastly, you should always remember that online trading is risky as with any offline investment scheme. You should thus only invest in money that you can afford to lose without offsetting your financial situation.

53

Online Trading System

Online trading system, there exists online trading systems in today's world, but one needs to do a comprehensive search of the online systems that will address the clients' needs and requirements.

The potential clients need to actively know that there are scandalous trading systems that will definitely rip the clients off. An accurate trading system has specific features that will transform any client's desires to a reality.

One-on-one training

The effective Online System has free support for all of its clients so that online account holders can operate them with the required ease and without inconveniences. The accurate online systems make sure that the clients' funds are safe and secure. There are scams that has marked today's world and therefore one should explore an avenue that reflects positivity and reliability.

Training is an important aspect of an effective trading system. It should provide a one-on-one training to all its users. Its effective in rendering a solution to online markets as far as trading is concerned.

An all-inclusive market analysis

An all-inclusive market analysis is the priority of these online systems. The clients will therefore make informed online decisions that pertains their trading endeavors. The trading system needs to be regulated to make sure that they meet all specifications and requirements to operate a trading system.

It's good to choose a trading system that has operated for a reasonable time period. This would be the ultimate test for a system that will deliver results. It performs an in-depth analysis of the market performance. The clients' decisions will be precise. The clients are better placed to make online trading decisions.

The trading system has a web based and mobile solution that is both downloadable and carries with it a fast execution approach. The fact that there so many phone users in the world today provides the most effective online trading approach. A trading system that has a phone application to its website will make the clients' transaction easy and dependable.

54

Forex Market Trading

Forex market trading is a kind of investment which involves purchase of undervalued currencies of various Countries. The investor then sells the currencies when the exchange rated raises.

Therefore, the knowledge of foreign exchange rates is crucial in this trading. This kind of investment is risky and requires some complicated calculations. However, here are some strategies for trading that may guide you.

The popular and easy strategy for trading is following the trends of prices. This strategy involves analyzing the trend of prior prices for a given currency.

Drawing a trend line

The simplest way to do this is by drawing a trend line which guides you into determining whether the trend is going down or upward. Some Forex trading software provides tools that aids in drawing the trend lines. Never purchases a currency which is not trending or is down trending.

Another strategy for trading is use of candlestick. A candle stick resembles a convectional bar chart, but it signifies the opening and closing prices of currencies at a given period.

The patterns formed by these candle stick helps the trader to make predictions concerning the prices of a particular currency. A simple pattern that you can follow to determine a significant turnaround in prices is the engulfing pattern. This pattern should alert you that there might be a further price changes.

Moving average is a technical strategy

Moving average is a technical strategy for Forex trading that trader has found important. It requires that you calculate the average of the historical prices of currencies for a particular time frame.

The averages are connected to form a line which helps to indicate the movement of the prices of the currency. When you find that the average is moving upwards, this should signal that the price of the currency is raising and a purchase option should be executed.

These are the proven strategies for Forex market trading, but great care should be taken since no strategy guarantees a 100 percent sure. Losses are often common if one fails to remain alert. It is advisable to study all the three methods and choose the one that seem workable for you.

55

Forex Trading

Forex trading is usually viewed by amateurs to be complex. However, similar to any other businesses, novices are prepared to be able to get into the business with the right techniques and the right attitude.

The forex market had anticipated methods specifically for beginners who wish to try their hands trading. It is only the initiative of the trader to find out how he could get into those methods if he is decided after all to earn in the forex market.

Forex market is ever ready with courses to train their participants. This is to prevent individuals from falling into the pit of going directly to the actual trading without any knowledge of what lies ahead.

You can participate

If you have the motivation, you can participate on the online training courses. However if you think you needed some forms of encouragement, offline training is best for you. Whether the training is offline or online, you are advised to do the free demonstration which is a necessity to test if you have learned something from your training courses.

Having the knowledge is not enough to thrive in the forex market, but rather a combination of both knowledge and skills. Once these are mastered, earning from the forex market would not be elusive.

As an amateur

As an amateur, you should also allow yourself to be mentored by the experienced traders. This is very helpful because there are still things you might need to learn which was not covered in your training. Since most mentors are experts in their own right, tips you get from them could serve you in the long run.

Mentors are not readily available though just like commodities in the market. You need to seek for them and anticipate their service is not for free. They are paid. Payment depends on the mentor as they have their own rate. If you are serious in your trading business, such payment for a mentor should not be an issue. Consider it as your investment.

56

Learn Currency Trading

Learn Currency Trading, with the current economic depression in the U.S. and many other countries of the world, currency trading is increasing in popularity. If you are interesting in getting involved with trading, there are three main ways to learn currency trading: 1. Consult currency trading websites, 2. Read currency trading books, and 3. Listen to interviews with currency trading experts.

If you want to get involved with currency trading as soon as possible, the best course of action is to start reading as much material on currency trading on the internet as possible. Do not hesitate to take this important step.

Maintain your motivation

It is essential that you get started as soon as possible if you wish to maintain your motivation and get ahead. Remember: It is not impossible for most people to learn trading, but it does require hard work and motivation.

After reading as many websites on currency trading as you can, it is a good idea to start reading books on the subject. There are a great number of currency trading books. You can find them in almost every library and in every bookstore.

New currency trading books are published all the time as there is quite a market for them.

Prefer listening over reading

If you are not much of a reader and prefer listening over reading, you should try listening to recorded interviews with currency trading experts; these are probably one of the best ways to learn trading, and are guaranteed to never leave you disappointed. Finding interviews is not especially difficult. Many online retailers carry CDs and tapes covering currency trading, and most of these can be had for a relatively low price.

I would not worry about the initial cost too much; if you are a serious student you are likely to gain back your initial investment many times over. Don't let a fear of failure hold you back. Start today.

57

Trading Spot Forex

Trading Spot FOREX, the largest trading market, across the globe, is recognized as the foreign exchange system. The daily turnover of this financial market is above $4 trillion.

The purest and oldest currency exchanging trading mechanism in the world is known as trading spot FOREX. This mechanism allows participants/traders trading actual bank notes in FOREX market against one another, oftentimes with unobtainable degree of leverage which isn't available in any other market. Global financial exchange system or Global FOREX was created in 1944 in result of Breton Woods Agreement.

This agreement was signed between victorious powers of World War II that laid down currently renowned over-the-counter, highly automated and heavily computerized Spot foreign exchange market. FOREX has bonded almost every independent country on the world map in this financial market, along with millions of individual investors/traders and thousands of corporations.

Like Federal Reserve Bank

Trading FOREX involves institutions like Federal Reserve Bank, European Central Bank, hedge funds, broker/dealers, large financial institutions and small-time retail traders as the main players.

Low transaction costs actually resulted in the involvement of individual traders in the FOREX market through online brokerage firms. Internet revolution has made playing in currency exchange market very easy.

A Spot FOREX pair is created in FOREX exchange system when one currency is matched by an investor against another foreign currency, for example, USD/JPY. When dollars are purchased in this example, equivalent number of yen is simultaneously sold for immediate delivery to dealer/broker.

Large-scale printing and borrowing

Brokers/dealers offer individual investors opportunity of making investments 50 to 100 times than their collateral for a trade. That's why Spot FOREX trading is very popular among traders. There's great potential in Spot FOREX market to expand in near future because of large-scale printing and borrowing currency by the industrialized countries to deficit spending. Learning and understanding FOREX spot market is necessary before diving into this huge financial market to grab your share of profits. Books are written by some of the most successful traders, can be beneficial as a starting point.

NOTES

NOTES

GOALS/OBJECTIVES